NEW ZEALAND
FROM ABOVE

First published in 2006 by New Holland Publishers (NZ) Ltd
Auckland • Sydney • London • Cape Town

www.newhollandpublishers.co.nz

218 Lake Road, Northcote, Auckland, New Zealand
14 Aquatic Drive, Frenchs Forest, NSW 2086, Australia
86–88 Edgware Road, London W2 2EA, United Kingdom
80 McKenzie Street, Cape Town 8001, South Africa

ISBN-13: 978 1 86966 126 7
ISBN-10: 1 86966 126 5

Managing editor: Matt Turner
Design: Dexter Fry
Editor: Brian O'Flaherty

National Library of New Zealand Cataloguing-in-
Publication Data

Wall, David, 1964-
New Zealand from above / photographs David Wall;
text Philip Temple.
ISBN-13: 978-1-86966-126-7
ISBN-10: 1-86966-126-5
1. New Zealand—Pictorial works. I. Temple, Philip. II. Title.
919.300222—dc 22

10 9 8 7 6 5 4 3 2 1

Colour reproduction by Colourscan (Singapore)
Printed by Tien Wah Press (Pte) Ltd

Endpapers: Dart River, near Glenorchy.
Previous page: Gliding over Lake Pukaki, Mackenzie
Country, with Aoraki/Mount Cook on the horizon.
Opposite: Mount Taranaki/Egmont.

NEW ZEALAND
FROM ABOVE

PHOTOGRAPHY
DAVID WALL

TEXT
PHILIP TEMPLE

Cape Reinga

Ninety Mile Beach

NORTH ISLAND

Kerikeri
• Russell

Bay of Islands

Hokianga Harbour

Whangarei

Kaipara Harbour

Hauraki Gulf

Waitemata Harbour

Auckland ○

Manukau Harbour

Coromandel Peninsula

Bay of Plenty   White Island

Mt Maunganui

Raglan •   ○ Hamilton   • Tauranga

• Cambridge

East Cape

Rotorua •

Lake Taupo   • Taupo

Gisborne •

TASMAN SEA

New Plymouth •

Mt Tongariro ▲
Mt Ngauruhoe ▲
Mt Ruapehu ▲

Mt Taranaki ▲

Hawke Bay

• Napier

Hastings •   Cape Kidnappers

Wanganui •

Palmerston North •

Cape Farewell

Golden Bay

Tasman Bay

Marlborough Sounds

Masterton •

Nelson •

Picton •

Blenheim •

Cook Strait

○ Wellington

• Westport

Punakaiki •

Kaikoura •

Greymouth •

Hokitika •

Arthur's Pass

Christchurch ○   • Banks Peninsula

▲ Aoraki/Mt Cook   • Akaroa

Ashburton •

Milford Sound

Lindis Pass

• Timaru

▲
Mitre Peak

SOUTH ISLAND

• Oamaru

Lake Wakatipu   • Queenstown

Lake Te Anau

Lake Manapouri

Dusky Sound

Dunedin ○   Otago Peninsula

PACIFIC OCEAN

• Invercargill

Foveaux Strait   • Bluff

STEWART ISLAND/ RAKIURA   • Oban

CONTENTS

Preface by David Wall   7

Introduction   9

NORTH ISLAND

    Northland   14

    Auckland   22

    Coromandel Peninsula   34

    Waikato   38

    Bay of Plenty   42

    Central Plateau   52

    Hawke's Bay   58

    Taranaki   64

    Wellington & Manawatu   68

SOUTH ISLAND

    Nelson and Marlborough   76

    Canterbury   88

    West Coast   94

    Southern Alps   100

    Mackenzie Country   104

    Otago   108

    Fiordland   126

    Coastal Otago   132

    Southland   139

PREFACE

Photographing New Zealand from above throws up a unique set of challenges that don't exist with ground-based camera work. Concentrating on looking through a viewfinder, it's surprisingly easy to forget that there's little more than a car-type seatbelt between the photographer and the open doorway to the landscape several thousand feet below. What can't be forgotten is that there is severe wind, turbulence and engine vibrations all conspiring to make it as difficult as possible to hold the camera steady.

At high altitude in the mountains or in winter, the problems of door-off photography are compounded by sub-zero temperatures making fingers and hands cold and clumsy. The alternative – putting the door back on – means shooting through Perspex. It's usually scratched, curved, distorted and tinted, and will reflect every bright object in the cabin.

Despite all the challenges, few things are more rewarding than being given a new view on the amazing landscape of New Zealand, having the chance to see something that may be ordinary when viewed from the ground become extraordinary when seen from above. Or viewing wilderness areas that few people, except the very hardiest of climbers or trampers, ever reach.

The photographs in this book have been shot on approximately 100 different flights throughout the country, using both light planes and a wide range of helicopters. In general, helicopters provide a much more stable shooting platform and have the great advantage over fixed-wing planes of the photographer being able to ask the pilot, 'Can you stop please?', or even request 'Go backwards'.

Weather plays a huge part in a successful aerial shoot. Sometimes, what can seem like a perfect cloudless day on the ground is actually quite hazy at a few thousand feet, sucking the colour out of the landscape. Particularly in mountainous areas, weather forecasts are not always reliable, and conditions can change dangerously quickly.

This happened once in Fiordland when I was in a fixed-wing plane. In the space of just a few minutes, one or two puffy clouds turned into a grey ceiling, completely blanketing the valley we were flying down. It effectively became a dead-end and required the pilot to execute a tight U-turn between the vertical rock walls of the glacial valley, followed by some low flying along valley floors to find a clear sky again. It's times like these when the expertise of the pilot can really be appreciated.

It has been a privilege to fly throughout New Zealand with so many highly skilled and very professional pilots. I'd like to dedicate this book to them and, in particular, to those pilots who are no longer with us.

DAVID WALL

Gliders soar up the higher reaches of the Huxley River valley, to the north of Lake Ohau in the Southern Alps. In the distance rises Aoraki/Mount Cook.

INTRODUCTION

Fly in 2000 kilometres from Australia or 10,000 from California. Watch the green hills rise from the South Pacific, or ice ramparts lift from the Tasman Sea. Either way, this is New Zealand from above, Aotearoa, the long white cloud of sea-misted hills or snowy peaks ranged across the horizon. Whichever way you fly in, and whether you are a first-time arrival or homesick Kiwi, the sensation is always the same. These are treasure islands raised from the sea – and the last stop at the end of the world.

Although about the same size as the United Kingdom, the Philippines or the United States' Colorado or Oregon, New Zealand's remoteness and isolation make it unique. It has remained lonely, deep in the South Pacific, for millions of years. This distance from the life patterns of any continent, and its entirely marine situation, has shaped everything about New Zealand's natural and human character.

The country went out on its own early, drifting away from the ancient super-continent of Gondwana about 80 million years ago. As part of the stitching along the overlap of two tectonic plates, New Zealand has been shaped through the aeons of geological time by mountain-building and the powerful forces of earthquake and eruption. Volcanoes, thermal areas, alpine peaks and fault lines are key parts of the country's natural character. The centre of the North Island is dominated by active volcanoes rising above a high plateau devastated and altered by earlier eruptions. The 500-kilometre-long, ice-covered chain of the South Island's Southern Alps culminate in 3754-metre Aoraki/Mount Cook, which stands only 30

kilometres away from the Tasman Sea. Mountains and sea cheek to cheek cause high rainfall in western regions, wind and heat in the east, a pattern common to both of New Zealand's long and narrow main islands. The surrounding ocean keeps the climate moderate, though it is distinctly warmer in Northland than in Southland, which is 1500 kilometres further away from the Equator.

Before human interference, three-quarters of New Zealand below the 1200-metre level was covered in lush evergreen forest. And such long-term isolation from another land mass means that a high proportion of New Zealand's plant forms are not found elsewhere. Early isolation had an even more drastic influence on the character of its animal life. Before the arrival of humans, New Zealand had no terrestrial mammals except small bats. Both flying and flightless birds inhabited the ecological niches occupied by mammals in other lands. Among its flightless birds are the kiwi and the nocturnal kakapo, the biggest parrot in the world. Until a few centuries ago, the land was roamed by the fabulous moa, the tallest bird that ever lived. Today, natural scientists from all over the world travel to New Zealand to study some of the most ancient life forms on the planet.

The first humans in this rich land inhabited by birds came voyaging out of the sunrise about 800 years ago. Maori mythology tells how the great Polynesian navigator, Maui, sailed deep into the southern oceans and from his canoe (the South Island), with Stewart Island (Te-Punga-o-Te-Waka-a-Maui) as his anchor stone, he fished up the North Island (Te-Ika-a-Maui) to create a new land. The first Maori migrants who followed

The Kelvin Peninsula on Lake Wakatipu, near Queenstown. This little spur of land offers a breathtaking location for a round of golf; The Remarkables form a craggy backdrop to the lake.

The meandering Upper Taieri River, Otago.

Lake Quill, source of the Sutherland Falls, Fiordland.

him settled coast and plain, living off seals and the moa which ranged the grasslands and forests like avian cattle. Later migrations from eastern Polynesia saw the formation of complex tribal cultures based on horticulture and the harvesting of sea and forest. Vigorous and warlike, Maori created a society governed by conquest and caste. The strongest iwi (tribes) occupied the warm and fertile bays of the North Island, while the weaker inherited the colder coasts and uplands of the south. Although living within the limitations of stone-age technology and an oral culture, Maori took the carving of wood and pounamu (greenstone) to the level of high art and developed a powerful tradition of oratory. Protected by empty oceans for centuries, the Maori became tangata whenua, the people of the land.

New Zealand's isolation from the colonial expansion of European commerce and culture ended conclusively with Captain James Cook's voyages of the 1760s and 1770s. By 1840, British emigration to New Zealand on a large scale was imminent and Queen Victoria's government persuaded Maori chiefs to sign the Treaty of Waitangi,

ceding sovereignty to the Crown in exchange for British law and order, equal rights of citizenship and a fair system of land dealing.

The invasion of British settlers was mostly peaceful to begin with, but there could be no easy melding of the European and Polynesian values of land ownership. To the British, land meant private property, a new home and profit from farming. To Maori, land was imbued with a spiritual presence, their ancestral home under communal tribal ownership. Conflict led to war and the inevitable defeat of Maori under the weight of superior numbers. Introduced diseases, tobacco and alcohol seemed destined to finish the job. By 1900 only about 40,000 Maori remained of the 200,000 estimated to have inhabited New Zealand on Captain Cook's arrival in 1769. But Maori proved tougher and more resilient than minority indigenous peoples in other parts of the world. Today the Maori population has rebounded to more than 12 per cent of New Zealand's total of 4.1 million. In concert with this growth, there has been a burgeoning revival of Maori tradition and identity – Maoritanga.

Auckland's central business district.

The Bluff on Ninety Mile Beach, Northland.

British settlement proved destructive not only to Maori. New Zealand had lost a third of its forest cover during Maori settlement, and European settlers quickly set about destroying another third. By 1910, great tracts of forest had been burned and felled to clear land for farms and towns. The face of the land was both savaged and civilised. Though European settlers almost destroyed a culture and a landscape, they transformed wild forests into the most productive grassland farms in the world. Underpinned by a booming export trade of wool, gold, meat and dairy products, the antipodean colony evolved into a more egalitarian and evenly wealthy society than the one settlers left behind in Britain. Pursuing the ideals of freedom from want, equal opportunity and private enterprise within the scope of the common good, New Zealanders created a liberal democracy that surprised old Europe. In the 1890s, votes for women, social welfare and advanced labour legislation saw New Zealand described as the 'social laboratory of the world'.

Today, New Zealand is no longer Britain's most distant farm, an outpost of Western culture on the heathen edge of the world. Though proud of their multiple origins – Polynesian, European or Asian – all New Zealanders can now lay claim to being people of the land, conscious of its place and future in the Pacific. But to survive economically, New Zealand must always remain part of the global village, continuing to export its agricultural and manufactured products across the world – as well as a native energy, self-reliance and creativity that have given the world such talents as Sir Ernest Rutherford, Sir Edmund Hillary, Dame Kiri Te Kanawa and Peter Jackson.

Living at the outside edge has its advantages. Although staying in touch with the latest technologies and newest markets, New Zealanders have the value of distance. Here there is time and space to stand back and assess what is best in the global supermarket of products and ideas. Living in a prosperous, uncrowded, open society and a proudly non-nuclear landscape, it is not surprising that most Kiwis consider their country only a short step from paradise.

Now it is time for you to take a look for yourself. Tour New Zealand by air – observe it from above in this book

Route through Lindis Pass in the Dunstan Range, Otago.

Cook's Cove on Motuarohia (Roberton Island), Bay of Islands.

– and see how nature, as if to make up for the country's isolation, created a world in miniature. There is almost every kind of landform imaginable: plain and hill and plateau and mountain … fiord, sound, river and lake … forest and swamp, grassland and desert dune … island and volcano, estuary and peninsula. Much of original New Zealand survives today and it is this marvellous natural heritage – the qualities of a sparkling climate, empty spaces, clean air, transparent seas and rivers – that makes the country a Mecca for travellers from around the world.

But New Zealand is also a settled land and much of the landscape has been transformed over the past 150 years to serve the needs of a civilised society. Ninety per cent of the population live in cities and towns that have grown beside great harbours, such as Auckland and Wellington, or at the heart of rich agricultural plains, such as Hamilton and Christchurch. Most people live close to the sea, in a country whose coastline is longer than that of the United States, and three-quarters live in the North

Island. All the accessible plains and downlands have become a chessboard of fields for grazing sheep, cattle and dairy cows, and formerly barren high country has been turned into vast exotic forests grown for timber. Nearly all the major rivers have been dammed or controlled for irrigation and, above all, for hydro-electricity generation that lights the cities and powers industry.

Fly from north to south. Start with the long Northland peninsula, pointing the way to the Pacific subtropics, flanked by endless beaches and intricate harbours filled with history that are the refuge for cruising yachts and deep-sea fishing boats. Fly on south, to the dual harbours flanking Auckland, the sprawling metropolis that is also the boating base for the islands of the fabulous Hauraki Gulf. Go east to the gold in the hills and brilliant beaches of Coromandel Peninsula, and beyond to the rich dairy-lands and horse-breeding paddocks of the Waikato.

New Zealand's part of the Pacific 'Ring of Fire' runs from White Island in the Bay of Plenty down through the thermal springs, pools and lakes of Rotorua and Taupo

Ballooning near Methven, Canterbury Plains.

Farmland below Mount Taranaki/Egmont.

to the active central volcanoes of Ngauruhoe and
Ruapehu, the North Island's highest mountain and top
ski resort. Now you can fly on via the vineyards and
orchards of Hawke's Bay. Or west via the beacon of
Mount Taranaki/Egmont, New Zealand's Fuji. Whichever
way you go, you will arrive in the political and arts centre
of the country, the capital Wellington, decorating the
harbour that, it was once said, could shelter all the naval
fleets of the world.

From the hills of Wellington you can soar above the
wild winds and currents of Cook Strait to take in the
fishing and cruising grounds of the Marlborough
Sounds. Go further west to the fruit and arts and crafts
haven of Nelson and the unpopulated beaches of aptly
named Golden Bay. Or go east to the vast vineyards of
Marlborough before hovering over the biggest province
of New Zealand, Canterbury. Spread across the waist of
the South Island, Canterbury encompasses wide agricultural lands, rivers for fishing and jet boating in summer,
hills for skiing and snowboarding in winter, and the

highest mountains in the country for mountaineering
and adventuring throughout the year. When you cross
these, you arrive over the wild West Coast with its vast
pristine rainforests, torrential rivers and tumbling
glaciers. But if you go south from Canterbury you enter
the Deep South, the largest and most distinct region of
New Zealand with its great fiords culminating in Milford
Sound, the extreme climates of Central Otago and the
southern lakes. Famed Queenstown is its capital, and not
only of grand and historic landscapes but also of all
outdoor sports, whether for leisure or extreme challenge.
Capital of the coast is Dunedin, home to New Zealand's
oldest university, a distinctive Scottish heritage and a
wildlife coast of penguin, seal and albatross.

Soar like a hawk, glide like an albatross, don't rush.
With a bird's-eye view take in those brooding mountains,
those endless beaches and surf. Take in the colourful,
corrugating sprawl of the cities, the pattern of paddocks,
the skeins of rivers and the mirrors of lakes. What you
see happened both a million years ago and yesterday.

The far north peninsula is New Zealand's fingerpost to the tropics – next stop Fiji or New Caledonia. Only 10 kilometres wide at its narrowest point, its natural highway is Ninety Mile Beach (*far right*) – actually closer to 90 kilometres – running almost in a straight line towards the country's northernmost capes. Cape Maria van Diemen (*previous pages*) was named in 1642 by Dutch navigator Abel Tasman, the first European discoverer of New Zealand. Here the competing currents of the South Pacific and Tasman Sea wrestle around the headlands.

The blinding white shores of Parengarenga (*above*), New Zealand's northernmost harbour, are rich with some of the world's purest silica sand; this is shipped south for glassmaking in Whangarei and Auckland. In late summer, Parengarenga is the gathering place for thousands of godwits before they make their annual migration to Alaska and Siberia.

Cape Reinga (*below*) is the departure point for the spirits of the dead in Maori tradition. They are said to lower themselves into the underworld – Po – by using the roots of an ancient pohutukawa tree that still clings to the cape's cliffs. Today Cape Reinga's lighthouse marks the northern end of State Highway One that runs the length of the country.

The Bay of Islands was the simple but apt soubriquet British explorer Captain James Cook gave to this sea-drowned river system dotted with more than 150 islands (*left*) and wrinkled by innumerable bays and peninsulas. A safe haven for yachties, it is also the centre for big-game fishing, first made famous a century ago by US Western writer Zane Grey. The Bay of Islands holds a number of world records for catches of various varieties of marlin, tuna and shark. Many of the islands, such as Roberton or Motuarohia (*above*), plus coastal reserves, form the Bay of Islands Maritime and Historic Park. The small 'hole in the rock' island at the eastern entrance to the bay off Cape Brett (*top*) was humorously named Piercy by Captain Cook after a Lord of the Admiralty, Sir Piercy Brett.

The Bay of Islands is arguably the most historic region in New Zealand. It is said to have been first discovered by Polynesian navigator Kupe in the 10th century, followed by the migratory expedition led by Toi some 200 years later. After Cook's visit in 1769, French navigator Marion du Fresne's stay in the area in 1772 ended disastrously when he and 26 of his crew were massacred, leading to the surviving crew killing 200–300 Maori in retaliation.

The earliest European settlers in New Zealand established the first mission station at Kerikeri and the mission house (1821–22) is New Zealand's oldest building (*bottom, left*). The stone store to its left dates from the 1830s. At the same time Kororareka, or Russell (*bottom, far right*), developed as the base for whalers and traders from all over the Pacific and became known as a 'hell hole', notorious for its licentiousness. Its growing lawlessness prompted missionaries to lobby the British government to bring law and order, one of the forces that led to the signing of the treaty at Waitangi (*top*) on 6 February 1840 when New Zealand became a British colony. For a while the largest town in the country, Russell's importance faded once the capital was shifted to Auckland. It briefly became notorious again in 1845 when chief Hone Heke cut down the British flagpole four times in a challenge to colonial authority. The later sacking and burning of the town by Maori turned it into a backwater.

The Queen City, City of Sails, City of Volcanoes, Capital of Polynesia, Auckland was first known as Tamaki-makau-rau, 'Tamaki of the Hundred Lovers', by Maori who coveted the rich lands between two oceans. The extinct volcanic cones that figure the landscape, such as North Head (*top right*) at the entrance to Auckland's harbour, were fortified by Maori tribes controlling the sea and land routes channelled by the isthmus. In legend, the crater of Lake Pupuke in Takapuna (*bottom right*) was the resting place of Rangitoto before it re-emerged offshore as the graceful island – at top – which dominates the approaches to the city. After the signing of the Treaty of Waitangi in 1840, Governor William Hobson chose Tamaki-makau-rau as the new site for New Zealand's capital. It had a good port on the Waitemata Harbour and was close to the internal waterways of the Kaipara and Manukau Harbours. It was also central to the densest population of the time, mostly Maori. Although the capital later shifted to Wellington, Hobson's vision has remained true. Auckland is far and away New Zealand's biggest urban centre, with a third of the country's people, and still hosts its biggest Maori and Polynesian population.

Within easy reach of the city centre are some 25 regional parks such as Wenderholm, to the north (*far left*), which provide a natural environment for city dwellers seeking relaxation in swimming, boating, picnics and bush walks.

A view out over central Auckland and the Waitemata is dominated by Westhaven Marina, flanked by State Highway 1 and the highly sought-after residences of St Marys Bay. Beyond the marina can be seen the 'tank farm' of petrochemical containers lining Wynyard Point, followed by the Viaduct Basin and the bustling wharves that lie off Quay Street. Overlooking all are the Sky Tower and the skyscrapers of the central business district. Everywhere, at any time of year, there are boats. The City of Sails is New Zealand's capital for yachting and boating, and Westhaven is one of the southern hemisphere's largest marinas, with more than 1400 marina berths and several hundred pile moorings. The marina's matchless location makes it the ideal base for cruising the islands and bays of the Hauraki Gulf as well as the intricacies of the Waitemata Harbour. By arrangement with the Crown, in 2004 Auckland City Council bought Westhaven from Ports of Auckland Ltd for $46 million. The Council's hand can also be seen in the recent redevelopment of the Viaduct Basin (former home of the America's Cup bases) and the ferry terminal, which has helped to make the central waterfront such a drawcard for visitors as well as a vibrant place in which to live and work.

As New Zealand's commercial, industrial and service centre, Auckland is the gateway for overseas travellers, whether arriving by air or by cruise ships and yachts that dock in the heart of the city (*far left*). The centre is dominated by the Sky Tower casino and restaurant complex, and night life circulates around the Viaduct Basin, a haven for luxury yachts. The kilometre-long Auckland Harbour Bridge (*left*), opened in 1959, connects the two halves of the metropolis.

The Auckland Museum (*below*) stands at the crest of the Auckland Domain parklands. Noted for its Maori, Polynesian and science collections, it also functions as New Zealand's most extensive war memorial, with standing exhibitions covering the country's military history. Annual Anzac Day (25 April) services in the city are centred on the cenotaph below the main entrance.

Only half an hour by ferry from the heart of Auckland, Waiheke Island (*right*) has become a favoured Hauraki Gulf suburb for professionals escaping the city. Once a sleepy holiday resort, it now sports mansions on lifestyle blocks and vineyards.

Many of the islands of the Hauraki Gulf are part of a maritime park with facilities for yachties, fishers and campers. Brown's Island, or Motukorea (*above*), was gifted to Auckland by a former mayor and, apart from evidence of ancient Maori occupation, it was also the place where the city's founding fathers, William Brown and Sir John Logan Campbell, first settled in 1840.

Auckland's south-western harbour is Manukau, first settled by Maori in the 14th century. Like most west-coast harbours in New Zealand, its entrance is guarded by a treacherous bar (*above*) on which many early sailing ships and steamers foundered. On its north head, behind Whatipu Beach, rise the bush-clad hills of the Waitakere Ranges (*left*). The strong currents, winds and driving surf of the Tasman Sea constantly sculpt and change the character of the coast. The tidal flats of the inner harbour are the site for Auckland's international airport.

Auckland's western black ironsand beaches are hot destinations for surfers from all over the world. Piha (*far left*), 40 kilometres from the city centre, has become a surfing suburb with views from hillside homes of sprawling Lion Rock – once the site of a Maori pa (fortified village) – ocean sunsets and the endless march of breaking waves. New Zealand board surfing started at Piha in 1956 and surfers soon learned the sea here is not to be fooled with. During one Ironman contest, canoes were snapped in two by the waves. Muriwai is noted for its dunelands to the north and for its gannet and tern colonies (*below*). Tracks head from all these beaches into the bush and creeks of the Waitakere Ranges above; some lead to dramatic waterfalls, including Karekare (*left*).

Captain Cook was the first mariner to drop anchor in Coromandel Peninsula's
Mercury Bay and go ashore to claim the North Island of New Zealand for the British
Crown. Now scores of small boats find haven in the estuary of Whitianga or tie up at
its marina (*left*) after a day of big-game fishing, diving or swimming along what has
come to be known as 'Cook's Coast'. At the Coromandel holiday town of Pauanui, the
'Waterways' complex (*above*) provides each house with its own private dock in a
modern luxury resort.

'Cook's Coast' is famed for its beaches and coves. Hahei Beach (*left*) is a popular holiday village. The terraces of old Maori pa sites are found at the eastern end of the beach, with high-tide blowholes beyond. Close to Hahei and accessible only on foot or by boat is spectacular Cathedral Cove (*above*), so named for the 10-metre-high rock arch that gives access to the beach. At Hot Water Beach (*below*) bathers can dig in the sand at low tide and wallow in natural hot tubs heated by mineral springs.

New Zealand's largest inland city, Hamilton stands beside the wildlife sanctuary of Lake Rotoroa (*left*), and also straddles the river that gives the surrounding region its name (*above*). The Waikato River is New Zealand's longest, at 425 kilometres, and has, since the earliest Maori settlement, been an important transport waterway. The river is the location for annual waka (Maori canoe) races and competitive rowing. Hamilton is the business and industrial centre for the rich livestock lands of the Waikato and home to the internationally important Ruakura Research Centre, a horticultural and agricultural research facility.

The Waikato basin (*left*) is one of the most productive farming regions in the country. Rich soils, copious rainfall and mild temperatures have enabled the development of high-quality grasslands that underpin a lucrative dairy industry and bloodstock studs that raise some of the finest race horses in the world. The Waikato's west-coast seaside town is Raglan (*top*), on the shores of a pretty harbour and estuary beneath Mount Karioi. The town is noted for its laid-back, bohemian lifestyle, arts and crafts and alternative therapies. The consistent waves of Raglan's Ngarunui Beach (*above*) ensure that it is on every keen surfer's itinerary, as is nearby Manu Bay with its world-famous left-hand break.

The Bay of Plenty was named by Captain Cook in 1769 for its abundance of thriving villages and the plentiful provisions he obtained there. Home of the famous kiwifruit, the region's fruitfulness also sees it produce much of New Zealand's citrus fruit and a wide range of subtropical fruits such as avocados, feijoas and tamarillos. The bay capital is Tauranga (*above*), New Zealand's premier timber port which handles three-quarters of the export logs from vast interior exotic pine forests.

The 'sea front' of Tauranga Harbour is the town of Mount Maunganui (*below*) with its landmark 232-metre-high extinct volcanic cone of the same name (also known as Mauao) and 20-kilometre-long ocean beach (*right*). The population of 'The Mount' reaches city proportions in summer as holidaymakers arrive for sand, sun and surf.

Active White Island (*previous pages*) lies 50 kilometres offshore in the Bay of Plenty and is the northern outpost of New Zealand's volcanic region stretching 250 kilometres south-west to Mount Ruapehu. The island simmers with boiling pools, steam and gas vents and has had numerous eruptions in recent times, including one in 1914 which wiped out a sulphur-mining settlement. Scenic flights over the island are available, as are boat trips and guided walks.

The heart of the thermal region lies south of Rotorua. Waiotapu (*above*) is renowned for its Lady Knox Geyser, triggered by soapy water; the Artists Palette – a hectare of silica terraces tinged with all the colours of the rainbow; and the effervescing Champagne Pool.

The Waimangu Volcanic Valley (*right*) is home to Frying Pan Lake, the world's largest hot-water spring, a four-hectare boiling lake known as the Waimangu Cauldron – at top – and the brilliant turquoise of Ruamoko's Throat.

Lakes Rotokakahi (*top left*) and Rotoehu (*left*) are among the dozen lakes of the Rotorua region. All were formed by past volcanic eruptions, most are the site of thermal activity and some are known for good trout fishing.

Rotorua (*above*), 'Sulphur City', has been New Zealand's premier thermal resort for 120 years, both as a centre for sightseeing and for those seeking spa cures and relaxation in its warm mineral waters. Many homes have tapped thermal bores for private pools and heating, following the practice of the Maori villagers of Whakarewarewa who have long used the natural hot pools for bathing, cooking and washing. Mokoia Island, at the centre of Lake Rotorua, is the setting for the greatest of Maori love stories, the romance of young chief Tutanekai and Hinemoa, who swam from the shore to the island to be with her forbidden lover.

In May 1886, tourist parties crossing Lake Rotomahana to visit the most famous 19th-century attraction of the Rotorua district, the Pink and White Terraces, claimed to have seen a fully manned Maori war canoe. Because no such canoe had ever been on the lake, it was declared an omen of disaster by local Maori. Ten days later, 1100-metre-high Mount Tarawera (*left*) blew apart, scattering ash and debris over 16,000 square kilometres and killing more than 150 people. Today it is the focus for tourists on foot, by air and by four-wheel-drive safari.

Lands around Mount Tarawera (*above*) and the nearby Kaingaroa Plateau, which were mostly barren after the destructive volcanic activity, have been rendered fertile and productive by the addition of fertilisers and missing trace elements such as cobalt.

The high heart of the North Island is dominated by the Tongariro volcanoes and Lake Taupo (*far left*), New Zealand's largest at 606 square kilometres. The lake fills the crater formed by several cataclysmic eruptions over the last 30,000 years, the most recent, around AD 230, recorded as 'The Fires of Tamatea' in the skies of Polynesia, signalling the presence of land deep in the South Pacific. Taupo's outlet is the Waikato River which, soon after it leaves the lake, foams as the Huka Falls through a faultline canyon. The town of Taupo is the centre for fishing, boating and adventure tourism in the region.

Turangi (*above*), at the south end of the lake, once a hydro town, is now the base for trout fishers casting into the pools of the Tongariro River, shown here running down to its delta. Rotongaio Bay (*left*) on the eastern shore of Lake Taupo is a haven for fishers at another trout fishing haunt, Waitahanui.

Sacred to Tuwharetoa Maori, the Tongariro volcanoes –
Tongariro, Ngauruhoe and Ruapehu (*above, left to right*) –
were gifted to the nation in 1887 by chief Te Heuheu
Tukino IV so that they would be protected in perpetuity.
The Tongariro National Park was formed seven years later,
making it one of the oldest in the world, second only to the
United States' Yellowstone.

All the Tongariro volcanoes remain active: the last major
eruption of 2287-metre Ngauruhoe (*previous pages*) was in
1975. Under winter snows, it stands sentinel to distant Mount
Taranaki/Egmont which, in legend, escaped to the west coast
after defeat in battle with the other volcano chiefs. At 2797
metres Mount Ruapehu is the North Island's highest mountain
and location of its major ski fields, although the 1995 season
was cut short by volcanic activity.

A hike around the craters of Mount Tongariro is a favourite day
excursion, and all features of the park, such as the central Tama
Lakes (*right*), are linked by tramping tracks.

The great natural sweep of Hawke Bay is interrupted only by the port and provincial centre of Napier, one of the country's newest cities. Although founded in the 1850s, Napier was virtually destroyed in the 1931 earthquake and its accompanying fire. The quake raised up extra dry land in what had been a lagoon and the city was almost entirely rebuilt in a 1930s art deco style which is now the focus of an annual festival and a tourist drawcard. Napier's waterfront, distinguished by its long row of Norfolk Island pines, is given over to the pleasure of holiday-makers with facilities that include a popular marineland and sound-shell concert area.

Hawke's Bay is the biggest pipfruit-growing region in New Zealand with the bulk of its apples and pears harvested for export. It is also heavily planted in market gardens which produce vegetables for canning on a vast scale. The country's second-largest wine-growing region (*above*), its vintage traditions go back 120 years. The wide diversity of soils and climate allow the region's winemakers to produce styles ranging from cool-climate sparklings to Bordeaux-style reds.

A winding road leads to Te Mata Peak, above the Tukituki River (*left*), the best point for viewing the orchards, vineyards and market gardens of the entire Hawke's Bay region.

The southern extremity of Hawke Bay ends in the limestone cliffs and headland of Cape Kidnappers (left). Maori know it as Te-Matau-a-Maui, the fishhook used by mythical hero Maui when he hauled up the North Island from the ocean. The plateau at the top of the cape (*below*) is the site of one of three mainland colonies of the Australasian gannet in New Zealand. Common around the coasts, this powerful seabird is noted for being able to fish by diving into the sea at great speeds.

Farmlands along this stretch of the east coast (*above*) often receive little rainfall and farming is only possible by grazing low numbers of sheep to the hectare and by damming scarce water supplies.

Like a high, white beacon, Mount Taranaki/Egmont signals to storm-tossed mariners in the Tasman Sea beyond. The 2518-metre volcano, likened to Mount Fuji, is one of New Zealand's great natural icons and has attracted artists and photographers since the 1840s. Dormant for more than 200 years, Taranaki towers over the dairy farms on its surrounding ring plain that produce a quarter of the country's butter, cheese and milk powder. The clean edge between farm and forest marks the boundary of Mount Egmont National Park, a drawcard for trampers and climbers.

At the ocean edge of Taranaki's volcanic plain lies the provincial capital of New Plymouth (*right*), founded in 1841 by the Plymouth subsidiary of the New Zealand Company. The scene of much conflict over land in the 19th century, the city now prospers not only from the province's rich dairy industry but also as the so-called 'Energy Capital'. Since the 1960s, oil and natural gas, both offshore and onshore in Taranaki, have contributed significantly to the nation's energy needs. To relax, many New Plymouthites travel 70 kilometres north-east to the seaside settlement of Tongaporutu (*above*). Far from TV and the Internet, they while away the days swimming, canoeing, fishing and reading in the kind of traditional holidays most New Zealanders have long forgotten.

The Kapiti Coast in the North Island's south-west is named for the bulky island offshore (*above*) that was once the stronghold for renowned Ngati Toa fighting chief Te Rauparaha. Today Kapiti Island is better known for being a predator-free sanctuary for many native birds who live unmolested in an indigenous bush habitat. State Highway One and the Main Trunk line follow the Kapiti Coast north of Wellington, and provide the road and rail connections that link the coastal commuter suburbs of Pukerua Bay (*right*) and Titahi Bay (*far right*) with the city's business and political centre. The predominantly steep hill environment of the capital has pushed its population further and further out to sites where suburban development is practicable.

The geographical, political and bureaucratic centre of the country, the capital Wellington (*left*) sits close to Cook Strait and beside the harbour that was once said to be capable of holding all the naval fleets of the world. It was these qualities that prompted the New Zealand Company to choose the site for its first planned settlement in 1839, confident of it being chosen as the capital. This did not occur for a further 26 years and, for much of that time, Wellington struggled with the limitations of its precipitous site. An earthquake handily lifted the sea floor to create more shoreline and extensive reclamation provided the land on which most of the city's central business district now stands. The links for road and rail traffic between the North and South Islands are roll-on, roll-off ferries (*above*) that make the Cook Strait crossing in three to four hours several times a day.

The marbled legislative wing of New Zealand's 120-member Parliament, completed in 1922, butts against the 1981 executive wing, popularly known as 'The Beehive' (*above*). The lawns of Parliament Hill are popular with lunchtime picnickers and Parliament's forecourt is the site for both ceremonial parade and protest march. Wellington's Botanic Gardens (*right*) are close to the city centre, accessible by the cable car, and feature the Lady Norwood Garden displaying 3000 varieties of roses.

Houses in hilly Wellington are built on every available site. Here, homes abut the road and shore of Karaka Bay (*above*) at the entrance to Wellington Harbour and cling to the steep slopes above.

Reclaimed land once used for vast railway yards is now the site for the sports stadium popularly known as the 'Cake Tin' (*left*). Crowds of 30,000 or more come to witness All Black rugby tests or one-day cricket internationals. Wellington's port facilities in the background are second only to Auckland's.

Point Jerningham (*following pages*) juts into Wellington's harbour, known to Maori as Te Whanganui-a-Tara, and shelters the boat harbour and prized residential properties of sunny Oriental Bay. The point rises to Mount Victoria, part of the 'Town Belt' that was set aside by the first city planners to provide green space in a cramped urban environment. Top left is Wellington's airport, straddling the often-windswept isthmus between Evans Bay and Cook Strait and likely to provide the most hair-raising arrivals and departures by air in New Zealand.

Long-drowned river valleys at the top of the South Island form the complex waterways of the Marlborough Sounds (*previous pages*). Pelorus Sound is adorned with innumerable bays and distinct side arms such as – at top – Kenepuru Sound. Larger bays are often the sites for mussel farms, but the sounds, and the crooked fingers of land that separate them, remain a paradise for boaties and those seeking remote holidays in such romantic locations as – at bottom – Waterfall and Mistletoe Bays off Queen Charlotte Sound.

Picton in Queen Charlotte Sound (*above*) is the South Island terminal for Cook Strait ferries. Road and rail head, it is also the prime base for Marlborough Sounds boaties. New Zealand's only Outward Bound school can be reached from Picton by sea or via Queen Charlotte Drive which winds around the bays to the head of the sound (*right*).

Remote and sparsely populated Golden
Bay (*left*) was named for one of the
earliest gold rushes in the 1850s. It
supplanted the more sinister soubriquet
'Murderers' Bay', bestowed after
members of Abel Tasman's crew were
killed here in the first encounter
between Maori and European in 1642.
Its name now suits the endless sands
of its golden beaches, none more
spectacular than the 35-kilometre-long,
sheltering sickle arm of Farewell Spit
(*far left*). The spit is a bird sanctuary
and buses take travellers out as far as
the lighthouse which marks the
northernmost tip of the South Island.

The track along the coast of the Abel Tasman National Park is one of the most heavily used of New Zealand's Great Walks, traversing beaches, estuaries and headlands between Golden Bay and Motueka. There are long-standing holiday cottage settlements at Awaroa Inlet (*above*) and Torrent Bay (*left*) but also well-spaced huts and campsites to cater for the visiting tramper. The broad, well-maintained walkway allows everyone, from children to seniors, to undertake the two- to three-day tramp which allows countless opportunities for swimming and sunbathing. The more energetic opt for kayaking trips which include visits to offshore islets and rocks along the granite and marble coastline.

The 13-kilometre-long Boulder Bank shelters tidal Nelson Haven and Nelson City's
harbour (*left*). Founded in 1841 by the New Zealand Company, the city was named
after England's naval hero and many street names echo his battles and admirals. One
of the sunniest locations in the country, Nelson is the centre for a region known for
its quality arts and crafts, alternative lifestyles and fruit and hop growing.
Baches (holiday cottages) on the Boulder Bank (*above*) are accessible only by boat
and are still used by locals who enjoy a simple, electricity-free lifestyle where it
feels almost like being at sea.

The Wairau River (*left*) winds over plains to the sea at Cloudy Bay in Marlborough, leaving behind an oxbow bend. The Wairau Valley near Blenheim was once deemed suitable only for dryland sheep farming until, just 30 years ago, trial plantings showed that the region was ideally suited for growing grapes (*above*). Marlborough is now the biggest wine-growing region in the country. Its sauvignon blanc and chardonnay wines are internationally acclaimed and the region is an essential stop on any aficionado's wine tour.

Hagley Park and the adjacent Botanical Gardens provide the 'green lung' at the centre of the South Island's largest city, Christchurch (*far right*). Founded by the Canterbury Association in 1850, it is the business and industrial centre for the largest agricultural province in New Zealand. The most 'English' in character of the country's settlements, its label 'The Garden City' reflects how once empty plains and swamplands were transformed by the planting of imported English trees and flower gardens. The city's Englishness is also reflected in the pier (*right*), built for promenading and fishing at the seaside suburb of New Brighton.

The early Canterbury settlers brought with them a Victorian Gothic architectural style which figured in all the major public buildings of Christchurch. The original, cloistered university complex is now the thriving Christchurch Arts Centre (*left*), which incorporates studios and shops, cafés, a theatre, a cinema and a busy weekend craft market. A vintage tram service connects the Arts Centre with ChristChurch Cathedral and its square (*above*) at the very heart of the city. The city's war memorial is at bottom right, Neil Dawson's sesquicentennial sculpture 'Chalice' at top left and the statue to the founder of Canterbury, John Robert Godley, among the trees at top right.

In the light airs of early morning, a hot-air balloon drifts across the Canterbury Plains towards the ski fields of snowy Mount Hutt, 2188 metres high (*previous pages*). The plains were formed from the silt and shingle brought down from the peaks and glaciers of the Southern Alps – on the horizon – by scouring rivers such as the Rakaia and Waimakariri.

In stark contrast to the plains and downlands east of the Main Divide, West Coast valleys are steep and gorged. The Franz Josef Glacier (*above*), in Westland/Tai Poutini National Park, powers down close to sea level, enabling tourists to experience glacial activity at first hand. Planes and helicopters carry skiers and expert mountaineers to the snowfields beneath the highest peaks of the Southern Alps (*right*). These nevees accumulate the snow and ice that feed the icefalls of such glaciers as the Franz Josef.

On its short, braided run, the Waihao River (*left*) drains the silted waters of the Franz Josef Glacier into the Tasman Sea.

The highest peaks of the Southern Alps (*above*), including Mount Tasman – at left – and Aoraki/Mount Cook, loom up only 30 kilometres from the coast. These icy sentinels rise 3500 metres above the vast rainforests of the Te Wahi Pounamu World Heritage Area, which encompasses most of the south-west of the South Island. In the foreground are the beaches of Three Mile Lagoon, which were the scene of a swarming gold rush in the 1860s.

Along the West Coast, the tourist highway that now rings the Southern Alps via Arthur's Pass and the Haast Pass was completed only in 1965. The saga of road-building through a terrain of bluffs, cliffs, dense forest, torrential rainfall and flooding is memorialised at Knights Point (*right*), high above the furious surf of the rockbound coast. Tranquil Lake Moeraki lies beyond. Not far away, below Arnott Point, is one of New Zealand's major fur seal colonies (*above*). Hunted almost to extinction in the 19th century, seals are now protected marine mammals and their numbers are recovering all along the South Island's coasts.

The Southern Alps culminate at the summit of Aoraki/Mount Cook, 3754 metres high (*above*). A sacred ancestor to South Island Maori, the mountain was first described by European explorers from the West Coast in 1846. Its ascent soon became a goal for mountaineers, but the first serious attempt in 1882, by what has became the standard route up the Linda Glacier at bottom left, fell just 10 metres short. The summit was finally reached on Christmas Day 1894 by four New Zealand climbers from the Hermitage Hotel. Although climbed hundreds of times since, Aoraki/Mount Cook's surrounding icefalls and exposure to westerly storms mean it is always a serious undertaking. Scores have died on its slopes.

New Zealand's second-highest mountain, Mount Tasman, 3497 metres high and almost entirely an ice climb, is also a favourite target for skilled mountaineers. Mountaineers here (*top right*) approach the summit via the peak's west shoulder, with a view of the Tasman Sea beyond. The base for these climbers would have been Pioneer Hut (*bottom right*), directly below Mount Tasman and perched at 2380 metres on a rock bluff overlooking the Fox Glacier.

'Towering in a massy parallelogram … far above all the others … no one can mistake it,' wrote exploring runholder Samuel Butler when he first sighted Aoraki/Mount Cook (*previous pages*) from the Mackenzie Country in 1860. Almost Himalayan in scale, the mountain bulks above its other 3000-metre-high neighbours and shadows the Hooker and Tasman Valleys whose glaciers once carved the land and formed the basin for Lake Pukaki. Pukaki is one of three natural lakes in the Mackenzie Country whose waters have been dammed or diverted to generate hydro power.

The second of the Mackenzie lakes is Tekapo (*left*), remarkable for its cobalt blue colours, caused by the qualities of the glacial silt brought down from the Main Divide by the Godley and Macaulay Rivers and suspended in the lake's water. Mount D'Archiac in the distance marks the northernmost point of Aoraki/Mount Cook National Park. Traditionally the Mackenzie Country has been a merino sheep-farming region, but increasing irrigation has seen the growth of cattle ranching and dairy farming. Its townships of Tekapo and Twizel are bases for every form of mountain recreation and adventure.

The third natural lake of the Mackenzie is Ohau, fed by the Dobson and Hopkins Rivers and guarded by the over 1500-metre bulk of Ben Ohau (*right*), known as Te Ruataniwha, 'Cave of the Taniwha' (water monster), in Maori legend. The road along the western side of the lake leads to Lake Middleton (above), popular with water skiers and campers and, further on, the Ohau ski field.

A glider turns over the high basins of one of the most popular tramping destinations in the Southern Alps, the North Branch of the Huxley River (*left*), a tributary of the Hopkins River feeding Lake Ohau. A hut at the bushline provides a base for climbs of the ice peaks around the valley, or crossings of the Main Divide at Brodrick Pass – at left centre. Rising above the Landsborough Valley wilderness beyond is Mount Hooker, 2652 metres high.

The Clay Cliffs (*above*) near Omarama are a rare phenomenon: pinnacles and ridges, separated by deep ravines and canyons, that have been formed by the frost weathering of ancient glacial moraine conglomerates.

The giant 110-metre-high earth dam of Benmore holds back the largest man-made lake in New Zealand, filling what was, until the 1960s, the Waitaki River valley. All the waters of the Mackenzie Country, from the summit of Aoraki/Mount Cook – in the far distance – onwards, flow into a lake that contains 50 per cent more water than Wellington Harbour. The Benmore hydro system is the key element in the Upper Waitaki Power Scheme, which is one of the key contributors of electricity to the national grid.

The main inland highway takes travellers from the Mackenzie Country into the Central Otago region via the Lindis Pass (*following pages*). Although 970 metres high and often snow-covered in winter, it is the easiest route through the rugged and harsh environment of the interior. The Dunstan and St Bathans Ranges stretch away to the uplands of the Manuherikia and Maniototo.

In a fit of imagination, Otago's first surveyor, John Turnbull Thomson, gave the name Aspiring to the shining peak that stood above all others on the Otago Alps horizon (*left*). Keeping up the romantic tradition, later surveyors and mountaineers named the peaks around the 3000-metre 'New Zealand Matterhorn' after clipper sails, such as Stargazer and Mainroyal. The high tramping way to Aspiring is the west branch of the Matukituki Valley with its idyllic bush-sheltered flats. Aspiring Hut – at bottom – is base camp for climbers attempting the high peaks.

The braided lower reaches of the Matukituki River, chief tributary to Lake Wanaka, are perfect waters for exploring jet boaters (*above*).

Following a decree 30 years ago to preserve its outstanding scenic qualities, Lake Wanaka (*left*) is the only major lake in the country that is not controlled for hydro power generation. Although it is the primary source of the Clutha River, which is dammed downstream, there has been no change to the configuration of its peninsulas, islands and bays since the first European explorer set eyes on it in 1853. Primarily the centre of a sheep- and cattle-farming region, the lake's township is also headquarters for Mount Aspiring National Park and a thriving outdoor recreation industry. Holidaymakers have for generations journeyed further along the shoreline to the Glendhu Bay camping ground for summers of boating, fishing and water-skiing. Wanaka's airfield is home to the Warbirds Museum from where scenic flights over the lake can be made in vintage aircraft (*above*).

Cromwell (*right*) claims to be further from the sea – about 130 kilometres east, west, north or south as the kea flies – than any other location in New Zealand. Once a goldmining centre and head of the Central Otago railway, overlooking the tumultuous junction of the Clutha and Kawarau Rivers, it now sits beside artificial Lake Dunstan, created in 1994 by the damming of the Cromwell Gorge. At the junction of highways converging from both coasts, it is also famous for its apricot, peach and cherry orchards, centred on nearby Ripponvale (*below*).

Between hydro dams, the Clutha River runs at full stretch for a while through the Central Otago capital of Alexandra (*far right*). Barren tailings – at bottom right – bear witness to the days when massive gold dredges scoured the river flats. Today it is better known for its fruit and wines, celebrated in an annual Blossom Festival.

Less than 150 years ago, the treeless shores of Lake Wakatipu (*previous pages*) were populated only by sheep and shepherds. Within weeks in 1863, the settlement of Queenstown sprang up as rich gold rushes brought thousands of prospectors to rivers and bays around the lake. Queenstown is now again the fastest-growing town in the South Island with a new gold rush of mountain and adventure tourism. Summer sees a focus on water sports, such as white-water rafting and kayaking. Winter draws thousands on direct flights from overseas to ski in The Remarkables – at top – or nearby Coronet Peak.

The clear waters of the Kawarau River flow from the outlet of Lake Wakatipu at Frankton (*above*) and several kilometres downstream merge with the cloudy, silt-laden flow of the Shotover River soon after it emerges from its gorge (*right*). In flood, the Shotover rises several metres as it storms through Skippers Canyon. Four-wheel-drive safaris take tourists along the hair-raising access road.

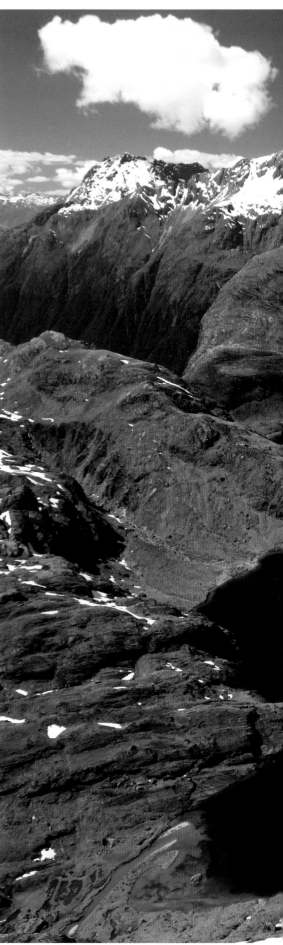

The Dart River (*above*) provides most of the water for Lake Wakatipu. Roads from Queenstown to the head of the lake give access to the sites of old greenstone working camps for pre-European Maori and a nexus of Great Walks: the Rees-Dart, Greenstone and Caples Tracks. Most frequented is the three-day Routeburn Track (*right*), which leads from the Dart Valley, climbing through subalpine basins around Lake Harris and crossing to Fiordland's Hollyford Valley via the exposed 1277-metre-high Harris Saddle.

Glory of the south, and of the vast Fiordland National Park, is peerless Milford Sound (*previous pages*). Dominated by the 1695-metre Mitre Peak, forbidding granite walls rise steeply from the surface of the sea-fiord, which is deep enough to host aircraft carriers and ocean liners such as *Queen Elizabeth II*. A remnant of the massive glaciers that carved out the sound remains atop the nearby Mount Pembroke.

The road to Milford Sound (*right*) climbs the Upper Hollyford Valley to the Homer Tunnel. For much of the year, the road is threatened with closure on account of avalanches from canyon mountains that rise up to 2000 metres above the valley floor.

Most of Fiordland National Park's 1.2 million hectares is a wilderness accessible only by sea or air (*far right*). Sculpted by ice, thrashed by metres of rainfall, and invaded by stormy seas, Maori knew it as Te Rua-o-te-Moko, 'The Tattooing Pit', an apt metaphor for a landscape cut and ground into an intricate pattern of mountain, valley and fiord. An aerial excursion on a rare fine day allows glimpses of hanging valleys, unnamed waterfalls and lakes.

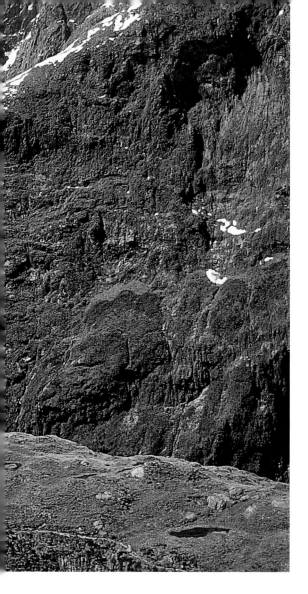

The Milford Track is the oldest and most famous of New Zealand's Great Walks. Every year thousands take the one-way trip from the head of Lake Te Anau and walk 54 kilometres up the Clinton Canyon, over 1120-metre Mackinnon Pass (*left*) and down the Arthur Valley to Milford Sound. Numbers on the track are controlled to preserve a unique wilderness experience and the route is closed in winter due to avalanches which may start as high as 1000 metres above the Clinton Canyon floor. The chief attraction of the Milford Track, and the original reason for its construction, is the Sutherland Falls (*bottom right*), the country's highest and fifth highest in the world, dropping 580 metres in three leaps from Lake Quill to the head of the Arthur River.

The two major lakes on the eastern edge of Fiordland are Te Anau and Manapouri, joined by the Waiau River (*bottom left*). Manapouri means 'Lake of the Sorrowing Heart', which almost became reality when it was planned to raise the lake for hydro power. A massive protest movement in 1970, which saved the lake, marked the start of the modern era of conservation in New Zealand.

The entrance to Otago Harbour (*right*) is protected by the Aramoana breakwater, allowing large container ships to navigate the dredged channel down to Port Chalmers, the biggest container terminal in the South Island. The Otago Peninsula at left is a haven for Southern Ocean wildlife such as yellow-eyed penguins and sealions which haul out on its ocean beaches. Taiaroa Head (*above*), at the end of the peninsula, is the only albatross nesting site on an inhabited mainland in the world.

Seasons are more distinct in the south, and once or twice a winter the Otago Peninsula and the Deep South's major city, Dunedin, are mantled in snow (*left*). Snowfalls also transform the fine gardens surrounding Larnach Castle (*below*) on the crest of the peninsula. More a baronial hall than a castle, it was built in 1871 by William Larnach as a retreat from the business of banking and politics. Among its outstanding architectural features are a 250-square-metre ballroom and a Georgian hanging staircase.

The heart of Dunedin is the Octagon (*above*), overlooked by a statue of Scots poet Robbie Burns and surrounded by civic buildings such as the Town Hall. Dunedin is the old Gaelic name for Edinburgh and most of the city's main streets are named after those in the Scottish capital, memorialising its origins as a Free Church of Scotland settlement in 1848. In true Scottish educational tradition, Dunedin was the first city to establish a university in 1869 (*right*).

Although most of the rail link between Dunedin and Central Otago has been abandoned, a section as far as Middlemarch has been retained to run scenic excursions through the spectacular Taieri Gorge (*far right*).

The Southern Scenic Route guides travellers from Dunedin along the Otago and Southland coast to Invercargill and beyond. The Nuggets at Nugget Point (*left*) are the focus of a marine reserve, rich in marine and bird life including seals, sealions and penguins. The coast sweeping north and south can be viewed from the cliffbound lighthouse.

At the southern extremity of the South Island, overlooking the sickle curve of Porpoise Bay, is the tiny settlement of Curio Bay (*above*). On its southern shore – at left – lies one of the world's greatest natural treasures: a petrified Jurassic forest. Overwhelmed by volcanic eruption, sea action has since worn away covering rock to reveal petrified stumps and logs of ancient trees lying where they fell 160 million years ago.

On the Southern Scenic Route, the Clutha River (*far left*), originating on the slopes of Mount Aspiring, winds its way to the sea near the South Otago town of Balclutha. The Clutha is New Zealand's largest river: although shorter than the north's Waikato, it carries more than twice the volume of water.

The Waikawa Estuary in Southland (*left*) is a haven for offshore fishing vessels, while the last loops of the Mataura River (*below*), where it reaches the seas in Toetoes Bay, are lined with the baches and stands of whitebait fishermen who wait to net the prized delicacy on the incoming tide.

The well-watered Southland plains (*top left*) have long been one of the richest fat-lamb and dairy-farming regions of the country. The Southland provincial centres are New Zealand's southernmost city, Invercargill (*bottom left*), and the nearby port of Bluff (*above*), which is the base for the Foveaux Strait oyster-fishing industry. Across the harbour stands the South Island's biggest industrial plant, the Tiwai Point aluminium smelter, which uses over 10 per cent of the country's power supply to produce 1 per cent of the world's aluminium from imported Australian bauxite.

Last, loneliest and, perhaps, loveliest is Stewart Island or Rakiura, 'Heavenly Glow', as southern Maori call it, reflecting both the island's long summer sunsets and the rays of aurora australis in winter night skies. The only settlement on the island is centred on Halfmoon Bay on the northern side of Paterson Inlet (*following page*). Most of the island is now a national park, protecting undamaged rimu forests and the rare native species, such as kiwi, which thrive in them.